gone bird in the glass hours

AGHA SHAHID ALI

PRIZE IN POETRY

THE AGHA SHAHID ALI PRIZE IN POETRY
Series Editor: Katharine Coles

  The Defiance House Man colophon is a registered trademark of
The University of Utah Press. It is based on a four-foot-tall Ancient Puebloan
pictograph (late PIII) near Glen Canyon, Utah.

Library of Congress CIP data for this book is available at https://lccn.loc.gov/2020001605.

Errata and further information on this and other titles available online at UofUpress.com.

Printed and bound in the United States of America.

THE AGHA SHAHID ALI PRIZE IN POETRY

gone bird
in the glass hours

a poem play

Zachary Asher

FOREWORD BY ALBERTO RÍOS

THE UNIVERSITY OF UTAH PRESS
Salt Lake City

Contents

Blue Postman sings 45

Act III: now the night heron

Foreword

by Alberto Ríos

One does not open a good book of poems, but is instead opened by it. That direction is the pathway through this energetic and simultaneously meditative book. This is not a book anyone else but the poet could have written, tuned as it is by a special ear and a distinctive take on experience. While these attributes separate it from the reader, it is a book one can— for those very reasons—enjoy throughout. It simply leads us.

This is subtitled "a poem play," and breaks into three parts. Among other ideations, Judaism, poetry, and love specifically occur throughout as major leitmotifs, each taking greater reign over a section. The references to these ideas are frequent and are themselves rhymes to each other, making the reader pay greater and greater attention as each reference builds on that increasing ease and familiarity of use. As the references and allusions to Judaism, poetry, and love accrue, they don't simply gather and remain static. They all are turned around in a kaleidoscopic manner, giving the reader an increasing sense of both perspective and depth. A poem play might also read a poet at play, but the playfulness is ultimately highly charged.

While tagged "a poem play," the inventive, compelling language expresses a volatile content that varies constantly, and is especially effective in its relating of odd or otherwise uninteresting things. The approach, including rhyme becomes incantatory. As these poems combine and build on each other, their language starts to win over the reader, and, though we recognize and hear the rhyming, the content is stronger, allowing sound to effectively underscore meaning rather than overtake it.

Though we might recognize leitmotifs, the collection is structurally eclectic, from whole poems to new couplings of single words. The word choices throughout the collection are good, plaintive defamiliarizations of the everyday. They provide striking language moments, are convincing imaginatives, and challenge us in their juxtapositions: "rabbi and surgeon," "bowl of bruises." This is all the making of energy.

One of the curious joys of these poems is the introduction of voices perhaps lost or going: Nachman of Breslov, Isaac Luria, Abraham Abulafia, along with poets and artists who are more contemporary, some with last names only, Neruda, Lorca, Rembrandt, and some as first names only, Sylvia, Galway. These references are intimate and historic both, a bridging of time and peoples.

Some moments in these poems enter the nature of feeling itself:

everyone here walks
like all our loves are far away

They ask simple and devastating questions:

how
to triage the darkness

And offer such human moment:

I've never been here before
welcome to hello

In this example and the following, "welcome" itself acts as a leitmotif, a rhyme, as a part of the great sense of these poems:

walk in, whether tiptoe or birdsong
your heart is barefoot, welcome

Throughout, an organic form of rhymesong emerges from these poems. They work in sound, in voice, but most importantly in sensibility:

would you rather be a jacaranda tree
come to brightness in spring, purpling everywhere
once a year until look now how you disappear

or an Italian Cypress
genus hourglass
who still lives
on my childhood street, pretendo, pre-tremble
aging parent trees
waiting...

Of particular interest in this example, and furthered in other instances, is the sense of words actually at the work of building, as if we have stepped in on them in the workplace—here, the telescopically extending "pretendo, pre-tremble," and in another instance, "afterdark aftersong." These words carefully construct their meaning, not finding it in just one word, and not in a rush to say it in just one word anyway, using instead a linkage between words, something not exactly rhyme, not exactly not rhyme.

There are various further good examples of taking language beyond the regular and using rhyme as the vehicle, as in this segment:

> *oblivious*
> *wow how*
> *night becomes morning*
> *when dawn comes down*
> *bathed in blue nightgown*

"wow how," so curious in its juxtaposition of short, abrupt sounds, leads gently to the later rhymes, most immediately "when dawn comes down," but with more to follow. In its stark rhyming announcement, "wow how" not only leads us to more rhymes but also suggests that the sound is both worthy and important. It says, bluntly, *don't stop here.*

Sometimes, the furtherance of ideas is seen in as simple as two words in significant company: "slaughter to laughter," for example. Here, we go from absolute terror to surprising redemption, all with the same set of letters save one.

Throughout these pieces, an increasing and usable vocabularium starts to speak itself. In these poems, words are simply needed into being— *needed* more than simply invented. They speak to a peripheral vocabulary, words that might have naturally formed historically, recognizably necessary kennings. The ancient architects of language simply seem to have missed these. For example,

> *blizzardburied*
> *pretendo*
> *breathspun*
> *hawkshadow*

Tethered to this sensibility of gathered new words is the use of good, fresh descriptors: "squint cold," "chocolate redwood," and more—all of this enough to be memorable.

Finally, we arrive at a purely ecstatic end, simply said. Along with the speaker, the far side of all these poems simply lifts the reader up out of the book and into the sky. Persuasively.

This book is, in sum, a voyage of challenges and compensations. I said at the start that this book led me—which also surprised me. I am always ready to enter a book full of whatever I bring. In this instance, I needed only to listen.

Chorale Personae

Rabbi
Vine
Ganesha
Sylvia
poetchild
Isaac
Blue Postman

Act I—Rabbi's Lost Sermons

Cleared for this
departure too...

the duskrudder engages you
your cut-
awake vein
untangles,

what's left of you, slants itself
you gain
altitude.

—Paul Celan, *aus Lichtzwang*

Blue Postman visits Sunday morning

And so it seemed
two cupped palms released
a blue eyed tree frog

into my wrist vein—
Sunday morning and cold.
Awakened by a ring

of high metal, the creaking
front gate dislodged
shema, so he does emerge

    Blue Postman

fired for scrawling ashprint love notes
on the lip of envelopes
   come to seal a letter in my mailbox—

old guitar in hand, he walks away humming like a child without eyes...

   omen or amen to open it
pacing the garden like an erratic
   spectre, frog-veined, a river

refusing to evaporate, kneading
my wrist for an underwater pulse
   —I opened it—

southpaw cursive, smeared ashes
in my own hand

    Dear

I am haunted by birds
crying forth from the wetmouth of God

one of which is you.

Rabbi and Surgeon over breakfast

I bury people for a living.
Still I feed myself

    and birds
kneel down, whisper to children

punch me. I have a stake
in the heart I have a shovel

what cut grass dreams about
    when metal scrapes bone.

    I eat breakfast

in the card shop café
with a bloodshot surgeon

this morning my friend
over mango macadamia pancakes

we talk about scalpels, angels
bleaching corridors, temple

shawls, anesthesia and how
to triage the darkness

we both tear clothes from the neck
    line to the soul—

instruments of survival—
fingers to heart, syrup to eyes

hydrating where no water is
    left behind, our stained hands touch.

notebook petals at the card shop café

these are the opening pages of today

                               I've never been here before
       welcome to hello

    hawkshadow on the highway
    blue heron who stalks the mind

                    trustpassing a bare field—*take it*

      dharma, lava
  the singular plural, let my breath be
     a whole poem

       . . .   . . .

     jacarandas be blooming
     late this year and now
     that it is late in the year
     my my May somehow
     young jacarandas are here

       . . .   . . .

was it before or after the whales
when you leaned into my ear
    unspooling all this pollen
and laughed a gasp in red stains
    thank you for knowing about yes
    love please, what shall we sing next...
even that night your song to my tongue tasted like chewing
    new lips, darkness

       . . .   . . .

God does not work in whispers
so when *HaShem* taps you, *ruach & duende*, gently on the shoulder
      you fall down

        . . .   . . .

Don't bury me in Burbank

where from the highway Mount Sinai
glows the bone hill green, wheels edge
a changed wind, where I hunch like *Zayda*
      hands clasped behind back
as Reb Tashlich presides morning candlelight
    he too once like our young gone friend
in recovery, hear him deliver euphemisms
for a fistful of multicolored pills like skittles
      aching gums eaten by the descending riddle...

    {for children's service}

would you rather be a jacaranda tree
come to brightness in spring, purpling everywhere
once a year until look now how you disappear

      or an Italian Cypress
      genus hourglass
      who still lives
  on my childhood street, pretendo, pre-tremble
      aging parent trees
        waiting...

           {tallis bag}

        keys pen hydrogen hydrogen oxygen
        tefillin atemwende celan this rhymebook
        chapstick painted yarmulke pocket jukebox
        pterodactyl god I need to write more
           dinosaur poems

   ...   ...

       what stranger, the poem
of faraway folk talking to themselves
or a strung narrative about grief again
      the right here real man
                      shooting children at school

   ...   ...

     Don't bury me in Burbank

where they float television pilots next to the cemetery
where my orchard is iliac joist *&* hair
where I pluck silken jacaranda leaves
     if any remain, and place them beneath stones
where my folks have reservations
     overlooking the endless / highway construction
where I remember the promise made
     in the woods, to the woods
where God does not care about the details
     yet was the first to cry
where mother *&* child are bowing to one another forever

       where I stand now
at the grass opened grave, biting my gums
     tasting sap, leaves crushed in my hand

Vine, would you rather be blizzardburied in a storm
    or hot day like today, effaced in sun?

      where the city boy
stares back at me through the leaf-wet ink
as I lift the hymns above my head like a veil
     a face without eyes, moai statue
a cavernous distance, where if an elder fell
quiet as dirt on wood, shovelful of sand in mouth
     he might not be able on his own to climb out.

bowl of bruises

Hobbled home from my little walk
to find the empty water bowl in the yard
   filled to the stars with black cherries...

cradle of glass, the upper half blown back
   to unripened dark, no chairs, nobody
found here—unbroken skin—bowl of bruises

   parachuted with green stems
or worms, or worse, bare hands *who left*
   this portent of precise care. Whose tooth

does not ache to sing into isinglass, the trans
   lucent sheet peeled off the rock, *and bite back?*
Tonight I am here and not near like you

   bittersweet *Vine*, dear wife, I am trying
to decipher the wonder, a stained poem
   without words from grave to grove

and survive with something to say in return
   for our congregation, *kol tov,* and my own
pelagic heart, all the gone blooming

of a weathered garden, nonetheless my garden.
   Of course I ate the fruit, then opened

my inner breast pocket with its gathering
   of pine needles, twigs, torn hair, the one
green stem, and spit the wooden seed into my nest.

   Tonight like all clear nights I pray for rain.

my god : carlights

set a glow in the dark bird wing on the bordering tongue
highway thirty east inside Skamania river gorge to spit myself north
  up Helen mountain : my god streetlights are bright at night : my god carlights

        … …

      and there she is
      the helixial blue
              dancer who twists
        the sky with eyes closed
          oblivious
          wow how
                  night becomes morning

  when dawn comes down
  bathed in blue nightgown

              & wafts you over
                  onto your back
          do you open & laugh
              with your eyes
                  do tiny sparrows climb out from inside

        … …

    young man heading home
    please give Michigan a kiss
            on the lake for me

Rabbinic Literature

An older gentleman
with weary skin who appears
to not have a home
often sits his back
to the record store wall where   [Ann
he sits his back now.   Arbor]

I was happening along   [State
after a midterm exam   Street]
in Rabbinic Literature

—one of those bright
cascading days, squint cold—

Eighteen year old schmohawk
sometime *menschlichkeit*
man he could sleep though
through the night that freshman
in a five student senior seminar
        why not?

My congregants laugh
when I say I am old perhaps
in their own own green but O
October I was younger then
& enraptured by once breathing
    actual mystics:

—Nachman of Breslov—
I don't care to remain lucid   [my Ukrainian Hart Crane]
in the midst of a people gone mad
        burn my words
but turn my tales into prayers

                        [tuberculos'd young
                        as kin Kafka, a century beyond]

11

Isaac Luria, Holy Lion of Safed
a man actually born / in Jerusalem, 1534
abi gezunt, his thoughts on *Tzimtzum*

   [withdrawal of God
to make room for us / broken vessels of primary light]

Abraham Abulafia, gentle Zaragozan
13th century, *unio mystica* meditation, my teacher.

But first this tall ligamental man
who still believed / in loyalty
who left the room *&* replaced himself
with a box of blue / oreos to proctor

                              [ancient flavor
                           the ones with the lard!]

We finished the first test.
Older pupils demurred the cookies
Oy tired, toothsome manners
   I took the oreos

on my walk home
where I happened upon
the beggar with his back
to the bygone yet operable
Talmudic Turntables—

      "Sir, would you like an oreo?"
         "Oh, sure, thank you."
      "Here take more, I have a whole bunch"
         "—no, no, One'll do."

Where are the unhungry hands old teacher
reaching out, a door ajar, all these prayers *&* years later

      One'll do.

one night it rained

mostly it is the way you brush your teeth
with a quick spit midsentence   *poof*
you finish the sentence   *poof*   you don't self-reference
   the spit.

        And holy it is how
        in bed you called me out
        for needing to summarize
        as if you weren't there
           in the fire
        you evoked the hedon-den
        not the ferryman quietly awake at the end
           but *Kamala*—

one night in Nashville it rained

                  [off with your heels]

        slip toes to asphalt
        you didn't complain
        because you don't
        and because one season
        you trained your feet
        to be able to scald walk anywhere
           anywhere   same as me...

breathing the body is practice
for leaving the body   still
you want to do what   *now*
           with all this pollen falling.

Instructions for Hibernal Solstice

This morning wake again
necked in sweat, go on touch electronic

buttons before toe to grass
before cupping thine own face

dear, let alone yours—left alone
     the sun, it shines

only so long, cherry-throated
like tanager or tongue
     bowing with the late wheel turn.

  December and the winds

make everything possible
branch rot and car parts

    you can move anywhere

if lithe, labyrinthine, galloping
ideas into body, minutes into monster

if you let yourself
be amazed, be a mare

not a mouthful of red
tongue-bitten shoulds.

  Open the dusky shed

      —carry down paint ladder—

my god it is
time.
      Walk backward to the yard

arborescent intimacy
O tilted home where
          green apples keep rolling off the table...

you can be moved
or removed
    anywhere.

December : string a door of lights
around yourself, unspool your eyelids

   walk in, whether tiptoe or birdsong
your heart is barefoot, welcome

to sand inside glass
witness or just bless

this new song to write
    because you showed up to hear it tonight.

It is not safe to change
the dead bulb

   old horse legs beat the abandoned mint garden

since you are gone, dear, vines keep appearing
everywhere wild vines
      berry the night.

Sermon before Bedtime

Please raise your young
daughter with a dog
and tell her one night before bedtime

    the dog will die
   sooner than you may
    be ready to say goodbye

will die when the glowering metro
gnome ravishes the rational
when gaskets wheeze or rupture

    leaving us
  bent like keys
        {behind God's bird door}

missive of cherries
or mess of chance
fracture / scripture

gematria or pi *I don't know*
why bad things happen to the light
nonethefall in prayer marrow

I crack windows : let the embryonic howl
pillow the larger pain I pray that
ignorance is not the same as innocence

    ...you sleep now...

forgive me this wounded crown
rapt with sugar *&* cane that blooms
bright tiny thing upon the skull

and when she wakes as I do still
with why's *&* eyes not quite under
    standing lean down and say

    because we borrow
every day even the air to keep us
    breathing because

the rough parchment of the prophet
said no child no mother no dog is yours
to own behold

    the night blueing
as it leaves   more space
    for music in the synapses...

Beloved of my broken
hope-lit garden, I tend to it by singing
    our daughter this song.

Heart Sūtra on Shabbat

Shema Yisrael   Adonai Eloheinu   Adonai Echad

Gaté Gaté Pāragaté   Pārasamgaté   Bodhi Svāhā

Gone Gone Gone   *O my Body*   Gone Gone Beyond   *the Gate of No More*

where all the birds have flown

afterdark aftersong   *Baruch HaShem*   where you are

beyond decision collision *&* the infinite curtain

stitching vein to *Vine*   lice to lace lichen   love to move

from poet to justice   worship to warship   man

slaughter to laughter   bears *&* prayers   abundance

to ambulance   naked to be named   from nowhere

to now here   widow lifts window   rabbi is river

devoured in vowels   *a dripping waterfall*   the heart's blue wall

where all the birds have flown

Gate No More   Beyond Gone Gone   O Body   Gone Gone Gone

Bodhi Svāhā   Pārasamgaté   Gaté Gaté Pāragaté

Echad   Adonai Eloheinu   Adonai Yisrael   Shema

Seeing Whales on Big Sur

with a borrowed line via Patty Griffin, Michael Dickman, Florence Welch

Because we climbed up to the mountaintop
    and you brought binoculars

Because we turned away from the buttonlight
    all that clever negative

and left for a while, let sweat drip off us *&* the Ventana cone
    rinsing our eyes

where for once wow we weren't too busy to come, or we were
    but came anyways

Because you asked me too, and I said yes—

    you can go blind waiting
    you can go blind waiting
    you can go blind baby
        O   sweet nothing
    . . .   . . .

Because we warbled like the passerine
    would swoop dive and return

with snacks and a line on the glottal stop between
    Grace and *Get Out of the Way*—

one of the few trysts to trust here on taken for granted
    damnit earth for what it's worth

we waited when it was time to wait
    carved stick to road when it was time to move...

And so we kept seeing whales from the mountaintop
    while I stood against a beating heart

chocolate redwood, swishing cypress at the crosslimb
        of forgiveness *&* surprise

I stood again, keeping nothing *&* unclenched—

     shake the dorsal fin
     call down the cormorant
     writhe in electric breath
          O   sweet nothing
     ...   ...

O how ripe it is to beckon the wetdark
        mirror terror

on a night when revelation is decision
        must bioluminesce my own mouth

after wailing long enough to taste the echo
        —whatever you sang down there

the Sleepless Vessel pauses a spell, believing you—
        so too the morning

warm again inside the walls
        standing under a dripping door

you can do exactly what
you decided underwater

        or write off last night's swim
like a dream either way there is not much more to say with water
        logging the song you nearly drowned for

stay or leave

     ...   ...

     you can go blind waiting
     you can go blind waiting
     you can go blind baby
          O   sweet nothing

Blue Postman returns by car

Every word has been said
one thousand times sifted & kneaded
beyond the flesh hold

by *Blue Postman* in his fission coat
carrier of compass ions & the torn apart
who stayed here to swab the passage

from this world to the next
like Avalokiteśvara is said to be
made up of one thousand arms

or Elijah sipping a house of songs
as a bird transformed into breathspun eyes
to see & sing the pure pain world.

Every word has been said
so now we drive

  my bluelimbed god & I

arboreal frog in the back
strum gums the old guitar

needled free of coniferous language
we clutch hands over the cupholder
—come, let us clothesline the twilight—

not stopping until we reach the sea or the blue elk

  throws down its glass horn
 for us to tunnel
 with swallowed faces
 together shutting
  the fuck up, mouth of stars.

Act II—correspondence in the glass hours

when I died. His eyes were
two black birds
and they flew to me.
I said: no—stay where you are—
he needs you in order to see!

—Sarah Ruhl, *Eurydice*

La Cortina Levanta : Los Ojos de Lorca

fractaled from Suites

In eyes that open

are infinite roads

are two crossroads

        of the shadow—

the dead always arrive

from those secret fields

                (gardenmother who breaks

                    flowers off of tears.)

Pupils don't have horizons.

We are lost in them

as a virgin jungle

              —the castle you come to

                yet will not return from

                  stems the road

            that begins in the iris

child without love,

may God set you free

from the red ivy

            now watch out for that traveler

              Elenita who embroiders

                ¡neckties!

Vine sings in the glass hours

First thing you should know
    about being up here is you can't

take your lake with you as eye ducts
    are always closed

still you will find yourself
    planting face into elusive glass—

where all the trees are packed away
    no birds no birds where I live today

where dead poets go when they are dead
    you can live here but you can't get wet

no slip prints   remember you are dead
    yet you go on

versing horses from the well without paint
    paiiin? who's to say . . .

nonethefall I am up here too on the owl ledge
    not knowing if you are

lover child bird or friend

        discovery or memory?

    Tonight
    I walk
    the paperless street with empty hands
    not knowing
    if I should walk
    forward or backward
        to find you.

outside the nun theatre

now bend the corner
to see come streaming
out of the small theatre

> one
> hundred
> nuns...

it was not glass dark
nor was it still dusk

> but walking rows
> of white cloaks
> with the neck stripes—

of course
　I tumbled close
　　had to

> ask one face

> how many
> she said ninety

called in a reservation
to see *Of Gods and Men*

> of monastic breath
> trapped on one
> Algerian mountain
> during war which is man
> jealous of pummeled sand
> *which war witch war more war...*

why yes I thought right here
a pure land of no men—

    Upsky my mind barks ha!
        ninety gods.

Ganesha enters the body laughing

Yes yes yes yes *yes yes I am* the Elephant God

      make room

inside your angry
bruised kingdom

      make room.

When was the last time you saw an Elephant God
or when was the last time you imagined yourself one

      mmm mmm for the sweet spell of it...

there is an absence to fill and yes
there are a lot of gods

      it is the temples my friend that are empty.

Do you remember Neruda?
what a bloom it was

      to sing through his body

Remember

      when he asked who
      cried for joy

      when the color blue
      was born?

      I did.

Dear Rembrandt

I am standing in your kitchen, y'know, your washing bin
I smell watermelon, wish I could slurp again...

    Just me now, everyone else is in the foyer
watching a woman, perhaps for the first time seeing her
mix powder *&* clay
          ...ohh wet paint...

delectable texture
the *davening* soil
      remember your house on Jodenbreestraat
in the quarter. You would've called *mashugunah*
on the first loud decades 2000, the techno ill
      logical future, from whence I write thee.

      Since you done gone
the fashion of the day is to wear the head down
      talus bone to eardrum
leaking caustic light out private digital cathedrals.

      We have forgotten how to live
how to wonder if
      wolves curve like your honeyed hieroglyphs
before all the buttons, gluttons hunching over glowscreen
      desperate to lift us to the moon membrane

and we have no gratitude
      and we berate the shit out of ourselves
            unable to sit still or turn one wheel at a time...

Blasted Pascal
as if I am one to speak

I write from a place
faraway as poetry
—tulip, now you kiss—

that dastardly *Postman*
   found me
lights off in the oven
   he swam up
stained blue with flowers
   I can't touch

        ...ohh sweet rain...

   Reb,

sometimes I see my girl's legs

crossed in the windowsill

   I massage her anklet around my wrist

it matters how the light streams in

all the way up here

please, poet of silence

a nun drew a map for me

to climb the yellow rope down

   to your basement, how did you learn to paint again?

     yours in the glass hours,
      Sylvia

Dear Galway

I watch you there eating after your reading
     on a blanched campus in Los Angeles so what

am I supposed to do, approach singing

     chicken salad, I love it too, old pickle
     see we are kinfolk, please pass the coleslaw...

but no
     body passes me a thing for I am crouched beneath
        this jacaranda tree
        watching you eat—

    of course I am carnal
    who isn't hungry, Galway,
    do the dead crave meat
    mercy, do the dead still sing?

At least today I am chewing
     the manila folder with five sequence poems

my own imagos in the purple dirt
     shook free from the freedom monster of memory

retelling a story of what
     actually happened, today

you engraved my *nightmare book*
     and I gave you my poems

gazing up at your flukeprints, my address
     today I don't smoke cigarette

and you didn't write back
     bless him, *poetchild*, not too good yet

Galway, did you read one, *one*
       of my mysteries, where poetry lives

and is a panicle shining inside pain
       where your cells sing

   climb darkness, or any tree—

      no matter, here I am
      so happy with myself

          for saying yes into the wind...

Today I am 23 again, everyone I love is still alive.

Stained Glass Tunnel : A Carson Cento

fractaled from Glass, Irony & God

Spring opens like a blade here—

    I took up the practice

        to breathe lightning

quiet as a bone when I come in

    goblins devils and death stream

    behind me like a needle in water

      I had no home

          in goodness anymore

ice radiates / a map of silver

    my sister's handwriting…

It is hard to find the beginning

    says the psalmist

on the day He was to create justice

    God got involved

      in making a dragonfly and lost

          track of time—

She is a citizen of the ancient

    and ravishing

        as an island she looms

      on tiny hooves

    long cold fingers

    dipped in blue roses

        pry open the red world…

Those who make pledges

in their sleep shall in their sleep

keep them

when she smiles like that

beautiful as all my secrets

aster thunder garden dark

Abraham, Abraham

a southern gothic after the binding

Sopping wet I return late
a night almost shattering...

near zero outside
    no snow.

I walked home arguing
with the magnolias

taunting them, not believing
they would survive
a winter sudden as this.

Colder inside. I can smell him

on our wing of the house
scotch *&* a bit of blood
mixed with lingering breath crystals.

He has done it again—

  moriah memory
grips the switchblade with my own
  sodden slackness

a narcoleptic slip *&* slap
      across the thigh of my jeans—

it is important I feel
the indentation of the blade,
what metal can do shaved

by hands made to be arrow fine
at the tip—the body, serrated—

Abraham, Abraham
I bragged to you when I bought it
 a spyderco delica

I made you hold it without sand
 here touch the jade handle

a paycheck, touch the cold thing
make it become warm.

What does a man pray for
freezing like this?

...afterberry deer lapping from the trickle
we once called a stream

where someone else once
ran upriver *&* begged
the magnolias to drain the excess...

 Father, Father
like the time you took us
 in a fit of tenderness

to the creamery and we slavered
 our first ice cream.

Tongue strum of vanilla
erased now by the glass
but I remember the absolute

glory of ice water, gulped from the fountain
 after snowing cream.

I pray for a lost deer
to stir a leaf so with my knife
  I too can scare something beautiful.

Mother of Laughter

Isaac, Postscript

If only we were there together at the break
dear mother I would say, slake your eyes to this
    bluecinating fog as it lifts
off the dolphin slick water like a ghost in autumn

surprising the light now, almost laughing blue
the color God as a child was when he was an ocean.

You would have liked him, my quiet new friend
    not quite awake once he told me
he saw a blue apple floating just barely beneath the bo tree

and shrugged it off in disbelief to the morning
    to seabirds scribbling, *this is the new day*
forgive the ones scrolled away, supine in the dark—

      How many nights did you live
      with Abram before I was born
      did you live how many nights
      before I was born did you live?

Before the three-petaled man divined a flower
in your gone garden, what with the summer rain
falling down, you named me Isaac, *laughing.*

      Imagine a god who comes down
      & leaves a necklace with *hot* letter
      burning life to your name imagine
      a god who comes down *&* leaves...

He called himself
Abraham now—
He who walked
the luminous blind road

lest we forget Sarai also walked, all day accessorized with a pocket knife
your design of long nights, joined with gemstone found, blue like mine
the only color still permitted here, so shines *good god* now Sarah

She who brought laughter into the world,
    She who dwells in the infinite possibilities of the seed.

Vine {reprise}

Turned off then turned on, everyone here walks
    like it hurts, like walking
    down escalator with the electricity

turned off—everyone here walks
    like all our loves are far away

so I tucked my teeth into a bowl of rice *&* gummed at stars

    lullaby, alibi

Tonight I walked where the birds were not

    and a tunnel opened or hands
    dressed clouds into my hair, alpine flyaways

    Up here

in the crevice, yes, where all wet paint is dry
    I find a playable version of my phantombody

    and sing from it

and blue larkspur briefly lights up the scarp
    reflecting my rhymes, calyx, thorn—

Is it still safe to stand here, up on this roof here?
    yes, you are no heavier than the rain.

Vine & Rabbi find each other in the ghost bakery

{somewhere like shasta cantalouped in fog}

Love please, we can't elope here
ground like cinnamon come dawn

> Let there be time
> when there is time
> like right now
> let there always be time
> for breakfast

Then I'll take a lakeful of yesses
with coffee & black cherries

> Viscous kissed ketchup
> for our omelettes darling?

> —pardon monsieur, don't trust the condiments in the cupboard
> the monsters under the bed put them there
> chimes *the grape ghost* rising from the icebox

Are there muffins up here?

> —grape muffins! plucked from the grape wide open

> ketchup ketchup
> pour it on everything
> the bottled red
> mystery of modernity
> clicking buttons
> ooh how we relish
> in fluorescent indecision

—anyways, I heard monsters *&* humans
disagree on expiration
dates, figs, oops when
come a kiss *&* do you want to
eat struedel with her?

Look at the curved fiddle tongues
collecting dew after the storm ends
the leftovers of rain, as in wake with me
stay, outside howling leafblowers

—may I top off your java, *Mademoiselle*, you hardly nibbled your stones

Hard to know
how long we have
to wait out the storm
I gain more
imagining the bowl full
the about to fall
rather than the bird gone

—may I ask you a question petite?

She seems to have slipped out
into the fog for a spell

—you then, Reb, why so terrified of the butterfly?

It is the lack of teeth
necessary to rip
through the density
of cherries or memory

—where do you go when it snows in California, where do you go
when the nighthawk, feet too small to walk, is afraid to fly?

I climbed here
through mud

                              —do you consider yourself then
                                    something of a hobbyist?

I like to watch
the yak-killer hornet strike
her tongue inside the hive
the juice becomes my mouth
    before this lake
    washes us away
where no ghosts dress me

                              —do ghosts often choose your outfit?

One time at crater lake
the sign said no swimming
    I went swimming
into liquescent blue the only way
    to describe is to imagine
    northern lights underwater

                              —did a ghost in water birth the butterfly?

It is the toothless texture
    joining the body
along the crest of the caldera
    where a wading friend
told me the first postmen

    used to deliver their dead

and ever since I can't dry off
these fingers waving hello
or goodbye not knowing why

the speckled pink blood of the heart
   breakingly beautiful butterfly terrifies.

Blue Postman sings

They came with sweet grasses, windroot
and dream recipes, veil whispering, *don't die . . .*
but the boy already coughed three days
red rain, upon being so close to the other side

and clutched on by loved ones
he lifts up, root rise to the purple night
in search of home. A child knows how to die
about as much as any of us.

I go after him into the Black Hills
not as others do to bring him back
but to guide a way there, help release
  bone gravity—

    at Wolf Creek I find him
crushed beneath half moon, where as a boy I was told
Crazy Horse used to ring his axe—
  say child, alone there all fire-twisted

what of the night? Startled back from where
he had just been, the wild thin bird body
takes off running, so I run with him, but he can't run long
so we walk, and as he begins

to lean and give himself, I gather him up
in my arms like flames *&* sing out
toward the blue light—*my child, my tiny spirit*
  of wandering love.

Act III—now the night heron

lift your voice like an oar into the darkness,
for all the sad birds are falling down—

Nothing in this night is ours.

—Brian Barker, "Lullaby for the Last Night on Earth"

you said the ocean

you said the ocean was the wailing
wall cried down into water and we
should ship our prayers out to the waves
the night we found a conch shell
and scribble-giggled each one a secret
note on a torn scrap of our empty
  lunchbags, slipped them inside
the siphonal canal, then buried the shell
in our hideyhole by the breakline
pressing hands to sand, perhaps to grow there.

Spilled a quart of life, diluted in half
light before I learned your wreck
lessness was not wielded by a rebel
lion, but a spiral tasting storm petrel
soon winged in the fury of your family
      dismantling—no time
to see if our prayers survived, you said
you would return one day but couldn't
be sure if you'd remember where
  we hid our hands, and would I still be there?

ii

double jeopardy
like a gull raised to the sky

sandy hook—
an open eye

friday, december 14, 2012

somehow tonight is still a night
resinous with news somehow
tonight is still a night with a moon.
     Afraid to weep we decry
warning signs   pills guns   pre&sub
scription to digital brain hate the fear parade...
     Come now tonight
too familiar too soon a night
for blame even while white he
     did make the small birds fall down.
Nor is tonight wholly a night
in praise of my president
who let himself cry on television
yet when he cried I cried, for this
     is about surviving
the bitter crack in the bridge
carved from Newtown to California
to somehow mend a family. I gathered
enough dream from this father
early Monday morning to offer
a blanket apologia from one head
of a synagogue classroom:

    I'm sorry my young friends
  you are afraid, I shatter too—
    I'm sorry we live here in a worse world.

tonight there is no yes

tonight there is no yes my god
they went fast—unagreed upon
dismal bargain left unsigned
to not decalcify inside the gown

pale varicose tragikos corridor
where the goat hips forget to hold
and you devolve aching into the tooth
    less time-lapsed abyss...

one way to say it : our children
are birds now, climbing a song
none of us have heard before, earthwhile
    this is our singing, America

produced by a herd of hungry ghosts
or goats tethered in the overgrown
heart's yard, bleating a thorny hymn
thrust into our monotonous mouths—

no thrush to rinse it out, for all the sad birds
    have fallen down.

how often here the horse

how often here the horse came clopping
at low tide to learn me the charge weather
she come to burden news or carry me away...

a start or a re-stirring, what mule, what shine
on the wet nape shovels off old hurts, baring
a mirror pendant or herself the missing rain

who won't die, who will glow in suffering
and is tender until touched. So few acts
master horse my hands know how to erupt

on *lavawhispering* earth : I know how to leave
soon as the craving claws on a muzzled wave
        and I feel claustrophobic outside

the opposite of ambidextrous, rhymeless
like an overfed donkey, I salt out a doorkey—
        to set life laughing again means to ride away...

look at the made world, culled by an ionate
creature who salvaged and sang yet who
went away, not needing to receive our praise who

        did not stick around long enough to revise our pain.

ancient hebraic debate

ancient Hebraic debate we debate
whether to light Shabbat
candles, Yahrzeit or Hanukkah *nerot*
    first—

all his aching acres of literature
about the dark dick of the night—

what happens when what happened
happened in the morning, the already

dead harpy descended and emptied
    his tempestuous feast—

  ladies of our protection, tonight no poetry will serve.

    Friday night on the birdfallen
        festival, *burn down this day.*

After moons of crying
tonight my tired sister
told me she is pregnant.
    I wept

convulsively, surprised my face could
stanch the spreading fire. She laughed

at the abundance of affection aglow
in the heat of her new body she made
no mention of the day's devastation—

O my lowercase candle, O my unopened i's . . .
    this, this is the world.

vii

driving to the synagogue
in the morning I pull over
muttering *justice* while birth
and death are joining hands

with my hands—through the window
I stare at the Amnesia Tree

who does not speak back
nor recognize me as lord
child or tree, I am returned
to the clan of the unmarried

{if this tree falls then this tree dies
no wren left to moss a memory}

I can stand on my head
with help from the wall
tiny feet crawl out the orb...
when I stretch my hips I sob

like a child, for a child
for my passenger seat is empty

headless even as I ride
with the head / rest removed
to see out the whole window
    O electrical ghost in the goatmobile

where I buckle my black satchel
to keep the sensor from shrieking body

    still instinct lifts my arm
into love's protection when I slam the brake
to keep the heart of my messenger
    bag from spilling the day's evidence...

still I keep brushing the sun off my sweater
wrinkled in the back seat, insisting it's a stain.

owl at the moon

what done

on purpose

in the ex

act moment

ain't martyr—

God of hour

mist stirring

who laws us

to live & love

who who will crawl

across the pearl

& etch your teeth

a waste of rain

ruin the peach

tear the flesh flag

off the moon

crepusculo caesura

elegy to the lifted refrain

for all the sad birds *who*

have fallen down

gone blues

everybodies rabbinate
everybodies ravenous

    & nerves nevered—

everybody gone have somebody
    to cry for *&* live on

everygone ghost is one crane
    who's gone   everybody gone—

everybodies ravages
everybodies damages

    & erasures come ashore

every vessel gets too hot to hold
every blessing is old

yet cleans one small wound
    every body falls

cause we walk   or sing across
    the green bladelets we tore

giddied up the horse and *yah*
    everybody god

washing body in the cold salt foam
    blue bones blue bones

& a tongue too worn to leaf
& a love too long to leash

    everybody gone

X

somewhere tonight a child
walks down to the water

to wash off some blood . . .

I'm sorry we have to hope
she's gone on   the volant thoroughfare
into the glass hours or beyond

where all the birds have flown

not here now here and if no where
fills the mind

then she must flower the heart
until it is blue in the sun

or not, or rot—

let her be there & be gone
be air & be poem

something brighter than this
a *bissel* in the wild abyss

it costs me nothing to bow
even if we still know not to what—

now the night heron
now the pure land
now the curtain pulls back

I don't know I hope
to wake unexpected in the accidental
beauty of being alive

with & without everyone.

conch prayers

whisper desperation   whisper love
even if we become   a breath
held longer than intended
      the sea rounds...

                    we are borne of the water, spun on salty lock
                     to breathe blue matter, it doesn't mean we
                  are given a boat back—so let me be a snack
                    & lay down for the churn, fog over the bay
                    let me be rain, an old dog scaling the sea
                     at low tide into funk froth, ready to swim—
                we leave home through one door, emptied away
                  the door moves—will you find it in time

      heavenly baker
let there be commerce between us
here, I will trade you a poem
for one of your rustic sandwiches
and I will understand your absence
     to mean you have yourself
a deal, but the pastrami will cost you
     a short story

                  love let her
                hair fall down
                  & thank you
               for watching over us
                     watching over the birds
                  love let
                her hair
           fall down *&* thank you
              for watching
                over us watching
              over
          the birds

the veil blue heron

the veil blue heron haunts to sing
as first light carves its silent ring
around the sleepless mouths now drawn
to curve inside the traceless dawn

come, scrape the mud, don't talk much
release one need beneath the rush
of crested air, let the sun blaze
your worn eyelids—shatter the vase

ashtrayed under all the mean jokes
   electrical magnetic freaks
   of anger and fried violence
where fun is not the same as joy

where hurt *&* hope compost the soil
   if we dig up worms, if we wail
for it scalds to burn down old fields
   to see just what our forest yields...

here a horse lapping creek water
so let us ride back up the latticed
   fencepost aswirl with lettuce
and licorice lacing the coppiced

   erotic root, the berry seed
deep in the ground, a buried seed.

         ...   ...

—look, if we are going to take off then let us take off

         our clothes   proof of hurt   our scores
         our phones   hourglass   oar scars

and run across the grassy horn section   where love is invention—

> for my gorgeous nauseous sister I believe
> in the foliage of the growing heart
> for the fuck & the untakebackable night
> for the uncoiled conch shell
> and the daughter of laughter
> forgive the happened and the unhappy
> for the songbook of the broken body
> and the dark hymnkeeper
> for the dead and the malleable not yet
> for any bruisable creature who says yes
> I believe in hope anyways

the way Charlie Parker played himself free
    shook clean from the Amnesia Tree

where not often but right now I am living
up here, would you believe it, with wings, and I'm not coming back
    so you'll have to pardon me

I've gone bird

echolocation

Celan invocation via "Freigegeben," translation mine own.

Blue Postman is a golem composed of Elijah, Avalokiteśvara *&* The Old Guitarist, origin unknown.

"Rabbinic Literature" is nested with twigs from *Souls on Fire: Portraits and Legends of Hasidic Masters*, Elie Wiesel (1972) *dayenu*.

"Seeing Whales on Big Sur" riffs — *Because you asked me too / you can go blind waiting / O sweet nothing* via Patty Griffin, Michael Dickman, Florence Welch, respect/fully, reverently.

Act II curtain rises when Lorca opens "Los ojos" de *Suites* (1920-23)— fractal translation *mio*.

"Vine {reprise}" owls a *lullaby* to Chance the Rapper, 'How Great.'

Plath pollinates "Dear Rembrandt" here in a 'country far away as health,' tulip sepal on glass.

"ii" pricks its wing on Margaret Atwood's 'You Fit into Me.'

"december 14, 2012" cries a bird call back to Larry Levis, Barack Obama, William Stafford, *air far*.

"tonight there is no yes" riffs on the Whitman / Hughes / blues spectrum, with an outro echo into 'Fog Report,' Audre Lorde, almighty.

"ancient Hebraic debate" cries a bird call back to Adrienne Rich a la the aureole of Ariel's wreck.

"x" bows & takes a sip at the pond of W.S. Merwin.

acknowledgments

gratitude to the journals in which versions of these poems first appeared:
Sleet Magazine, "Blue Postman Sings"
J.New Books, "notebook petals at the card shop café," "*Vine &* Rabbi
    find each other in the ghost bakery"
Juked, "Blue Postman visits Sunday Morning," "Rabbinic Literature"—
    thank you Michael Barach at Juked for nominating the rebbe for a
    pushcart prize
"Rabbi and Surgeon over breakfast," "bowl of bruises," "Instructions
    for Hibernal Solstice," "Sermon before Bedtime" published in
    sequence as "Rabbi's Lost Sermons"

thank you Hannah New, Jessica Booth, Patrick Hadley
at The University of Utah Press for the arcing texture of this book
    thank you Edward Hirsch, Traci Brimhall, Sarah Maclay
beyond blossom
    thank you Alberto Ríos for blessing the birds

for fellowship oar *&* feather dipped along the way:
Mike Dow, Paul Epp, Sam Miner, Natalie Ford, Ezra Fradkin, Genny
King, jon stollenmeyer, Rabbi Ed Feinstein, Killian Quigley, Kate
Daniels, Rick Hilles, Mark Jarman, joseph tepperman, Elizabeth
Covington, emie elea, Adam Rose, Alex Carver, Cosette Stark, Dave
Shojai, *thank you*

for Alana, Marissa, Andrew, David, siblings all
for Mama *&* Marshall, *shehecheyanu*
for davis cook *&* samson, tiny beasts of the light

amen